The Hippo Campus

The Interactive Brain Book:
Fun Learning for Science Lovers

The Hippo Campus

The Interactive Brain Book:
Fun Learning for Science Lovers

Helen Borel, PhD

Fresh Ink Group
Guntersville

The Hippo Campus

The Interactive Brain Book:
Fun Learning for Science Lovers

Copyright © 2017
by Helen Borel, PhD
All rights reserved

Fresh Ink Group
An Imprint of:
The Fresh Ink Group, LLC
Box 931
Guntersville, AL 35976
Email: info@FreshInkGroup.com
FreshInkGroup.com

Edition 1.0   2017

Book design & cover by Stephen Geez / Fresh Ink Group
Artwork by Anik / Fresh Ink Group

Cataloging-in-Publication Recommendations:
JNF051030   **JUVENILE NONFICTION** / Science & Nature / Anatomy & Physiology
JNF024000   **JUVENILE NONFICTION** / Health & Daily Living / General
JNF008000   **JUVENILE NONFICTION** / Body, Mind & Spirit

Library of Congress Control Number: 2017952403

Paper-cover ISBN-13: 978-1-936442-34-8
Hardcover ISBN-13: 978-1-936442-33-1
eBook ISBN-13: 978-1-936442-55-3

The Hippo Campus Table of Contents

The Hippo Campus

Helen Borel, PhD

Live. Laugh. Learn.

The hippocampus is really a place to remember inside your head.

It's really one word.   **Say: HIP - OH - CAMP - US.**

Although it's not really a college, your hippocampus is a very important place inside you. That's because it remembers things that happen to you and reminds you of them. And it does this for you without you even knowing it's happening.

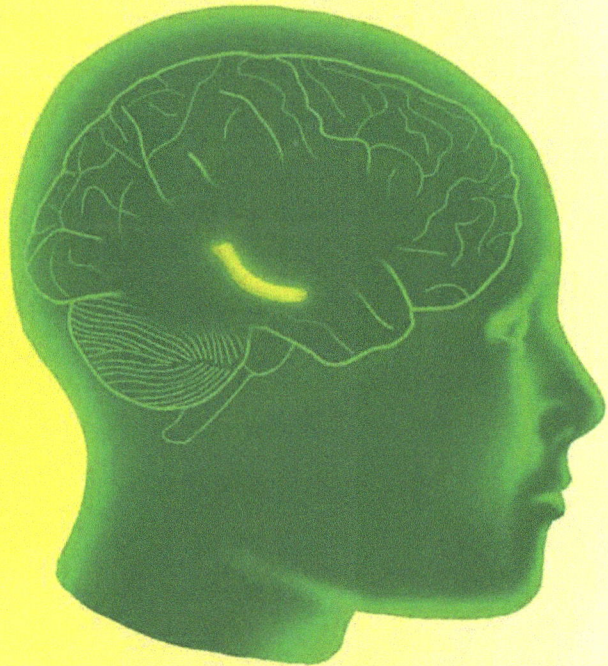

There it is. See that bright, curvy shape inside that picture? It's a seahorse-shaped place in the middle of your brain. It reminds you of things that just happened to you. And, it stashes away many other memories that you don't need to pay attention to until another time.

Say: MEM - OR - EEZ.

And this is your remembering book about your brain.

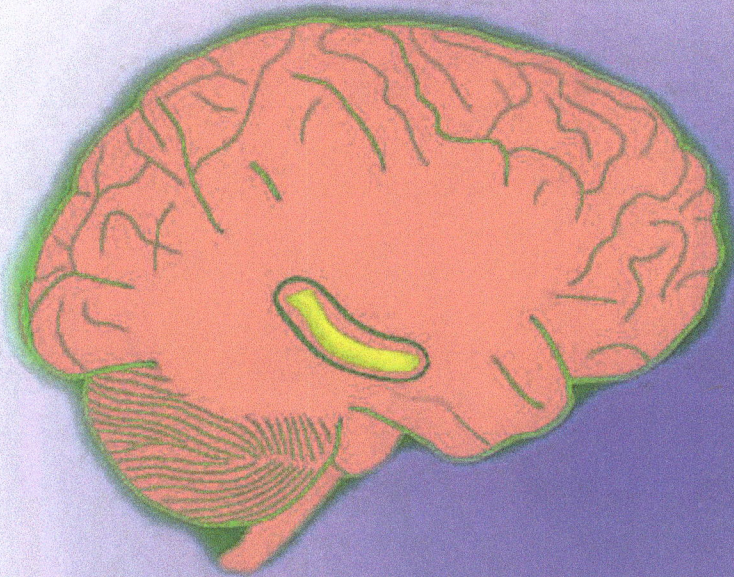

Your hippocampus is just one special place in your brain. And your brain, although a small part of you, is a very important place in you that does so much for you.

It also keeps learning new things all the time. So think of your brain as a place of many classrooms for learning many subjects. A place for doing many things. And for keeping, safely, all the many things that ever happen to you. And your *memories* of them... ready for you to remember whenever you need them.

Now, start your journey into many of your brain's places at *Your Amazing Brain.*

Imagine this!

When you grow up, your brain will weigh only 3 pounds. See how the doctor can hold a whole brain in his hand? But don't let its small size fool you.

You must remember this!

When you *imagine* something, your brain is making pictures of it for you.

Say: IM - ADD - JIN.

Your brain is an endless place, like a school full of classrooms!

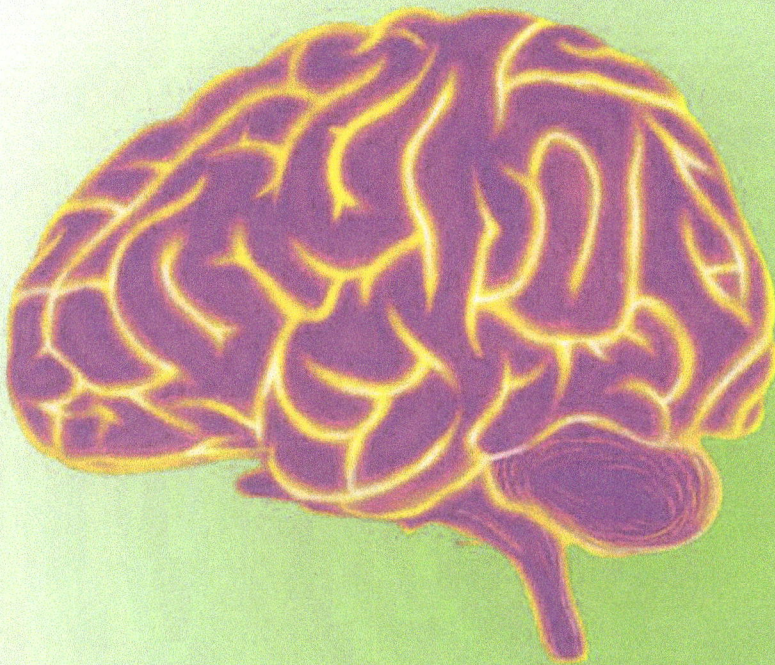

The more you learn about your brain, the more amazing places you'll find there. So, think of your brain as a college, with many special classrooms. There you'll never stop learning so many different things.

And learn about all the things your brain does for you without you even knowing while they're happening. Like the beating of your heart. Like the breathing of your lungs. And so much more.

Imagine that!

Your brain looks all _wrinkled_, like a _crinkled_ hat.

Say: RING - CULLED.

Say: KRING - CULLED.

If your brain were flat and without wrinkles, it would be stretched out much wider. That's because your brain is always learning something new and has many different things to do all day long.

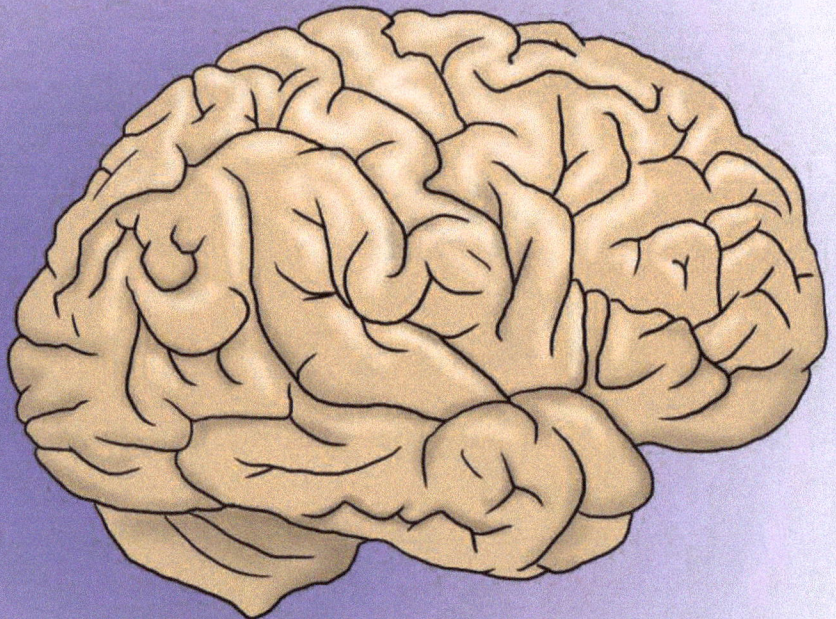

But, because it needs to fit inside your head, its wrinkles give your brain much more space to do what it needs to do for you. A special name for these wrinkles is _convolutions_.

Say: CON - VO - LOO - SHUNS.

Even at only 3 pounds small, your brain holds a universe of wonderful places and amazing happenings. You'll discover these in the coming exciting pages about your brain.

See how different artists draw a brain:

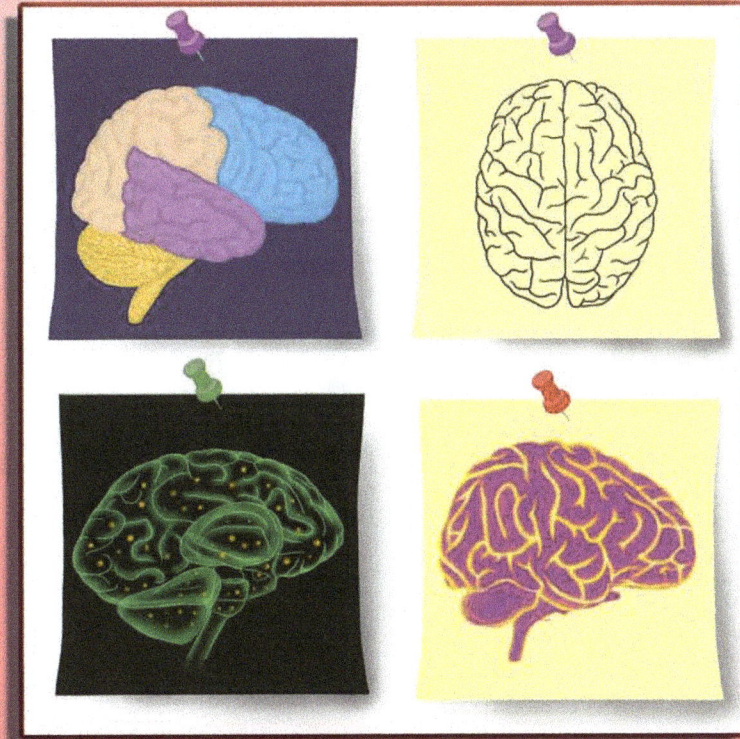

Now, you can make a brain hat out of a brown paper bag.

You can use crayons to draw the different parts of the brain you'll be reading about in the coming pages.

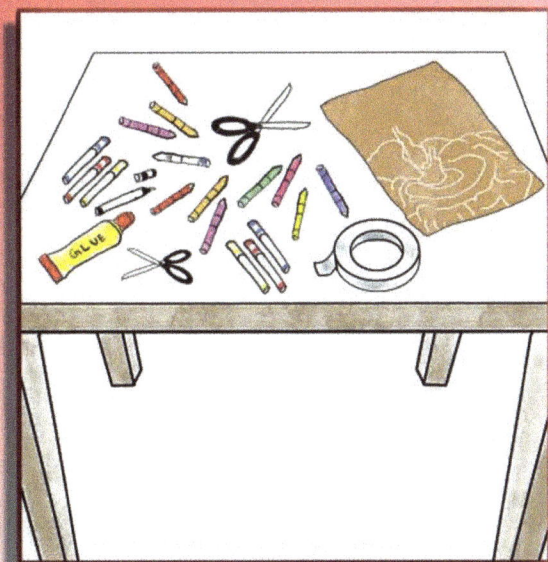

Think of those wrinkles as _thinkles._

Say: THING - CULLS.

Some people think that the more wrinkles you have in your brain, the more you are thinking, learning, and remembering.

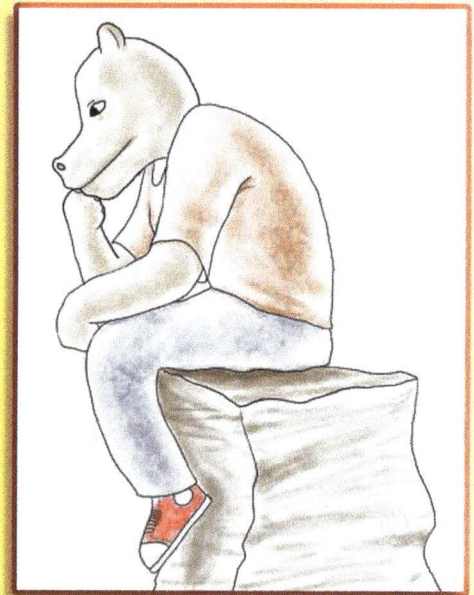

Thinking is important because it helps you plan what to do next. It helps you get new ideas. It helps you make music, art and inventions.

Always remember: It's a smart idea to think.

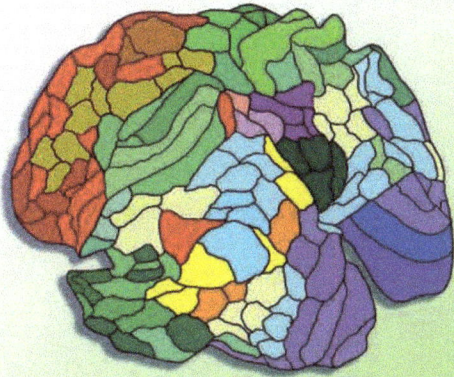

Your amazing brain does so much for you.

Walking & Talking

Crying & Tying

Reading & Leading

Remembering

Decembering

And your brain all by itself:

- Makes you sleep and makes you wake!
- Keeps every memory you make!
- Causes every breath you take!
- Beats your heart without a break!

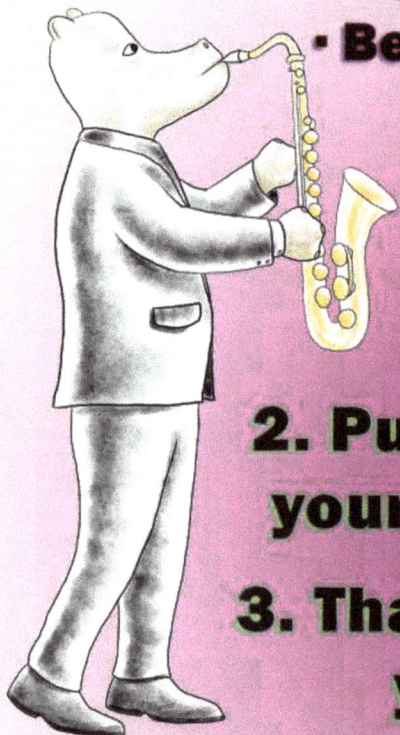

How to feel your heartbeat

1. Turn your left hand up toward the ceiling.

2. Put your right middle finger on your left wrist below the thumb.

3. That beat you feel is your "pulse."

4. Count how many beats in 30 seconds, then times it by 2 for your *beats per minute.*

68-82 bpm is good. Lower can be okay. Exercise makes it faster. Everybody's is different. Yours will be different each time.

Remember this:

Your brain is alive because of the air and sugar your heart pumps up through your body pipes called arteries.

Say: R - TUH - REEZ.

See what your heart looks like?

The blood in your arteries brings that air, called oxygen, and that sugar, called glucose into your brain.

Say: OX - UH - JEN.
Say: GLUE - KOSE.

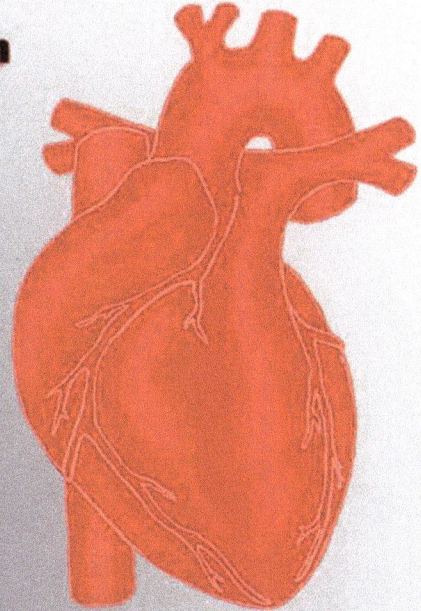

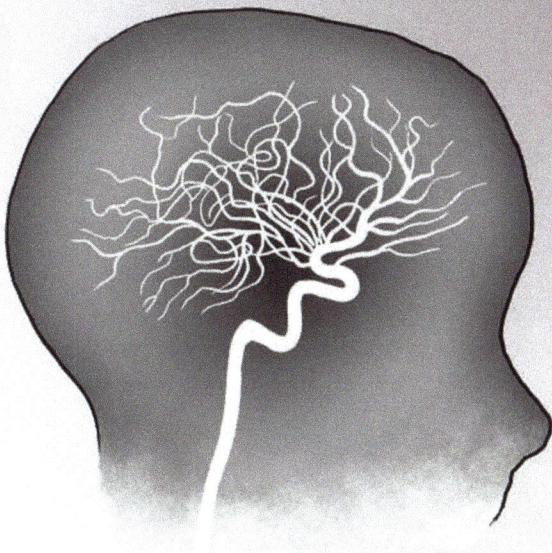

This is what your healthy brain arteries look like. Like branches in a tree, they reach every part of your brain. Like a magic highway, they deliver the oxygen and glucose that feeds your brain. Just enough air and sugar so you can walk, talk, think, breathe, laugh, love, learn and remember.

Your brain is alive

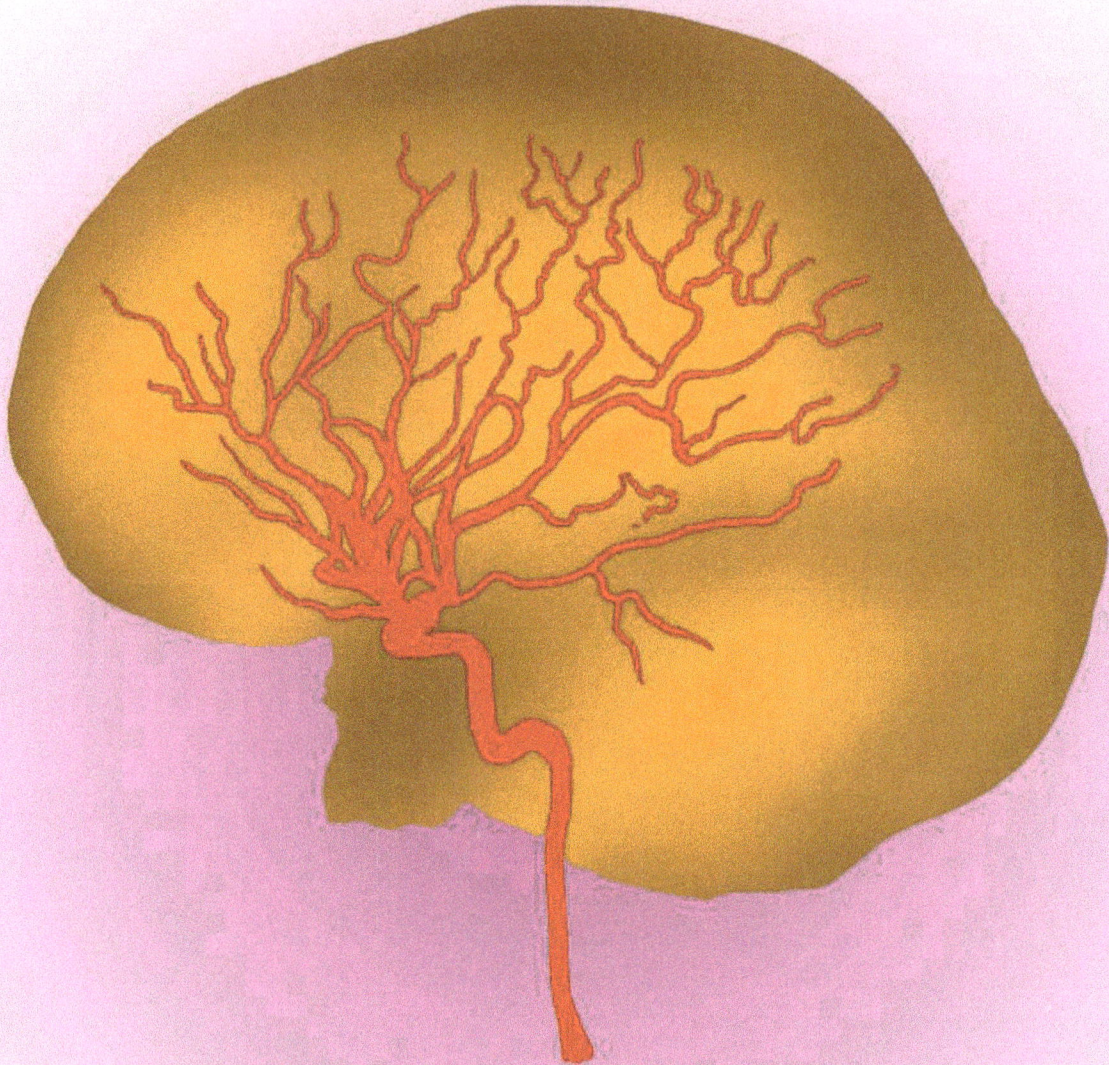

because of the air
you breathe
and the food you eat.

Food for thought:

All these foods are rich in nature's good chemicals.

Eat eggs. Eggs help you do well on school tests. That's because the *choline* in eggs makes a very important brain chemical to help you memorize things better.

Say: KOH - LEEN

Eat leafy green vegetables, like kale, lettuce and spinach. These keep you from getting sick. Also, they keep your brain healthy for remembering many things.

Eat salmon and other fish. These fish are rich in Omega-3 Fatty Acids that protect your memory and keep it sharp.

Say: OH - MAY - GOH - 3   FAT - EE   AA - SIDZ

Eat blueberries for remembering better.

Eat avocados.

Avocados feed your brain healthy oils that help your blood flow smoothly through your brain. This feeds your brain more *oxygen* and more *glucose*.

Again, look back at Remember This. See your brain's blood flowing smoothly in that colorful brain picture? Always remember, it carries your oxygen and glucose to all those many brain places you will be learning about in this brain book.

You should *eat walnuts* because they are full of Vitamin E, which also keeps your brain healthy and your memory sharp.

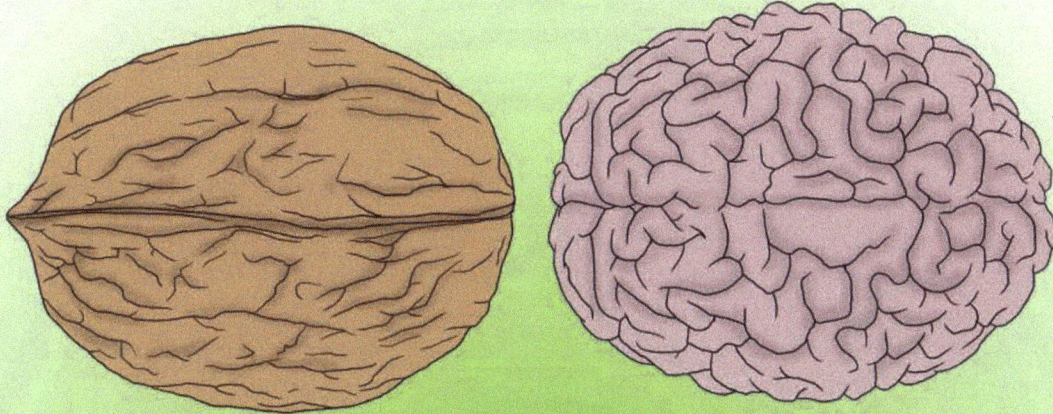

Look closely.

Can you see something special about a walnut? And its shell? Wow! The walnut shell looks just like the wrinkles, crinkles, thinkles of your brain. And so does the walnut itself. Isn't it amazing that walnuts are healthy for your brain and they look like your brain too?

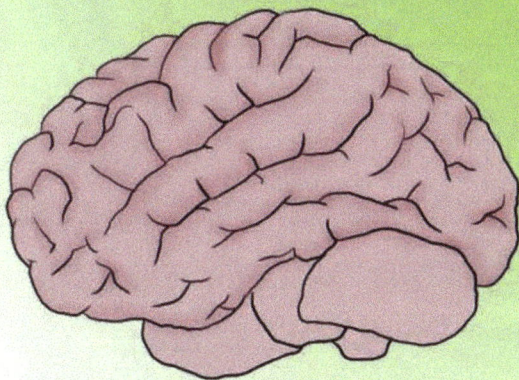

Do you want a healthy brain?

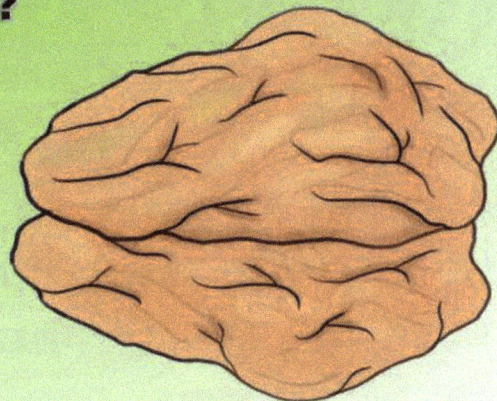

Remember to eat brain-healthy foods.

Your brain is like a school inside your head.

Pretend you're inside this make-believe brain. Find the science class. Find the music room. Find the library. Find the cooking class.

Your brain is where you learn and remember.

Your brain has two separate parts: Your right lobe and your left lobe.

It's like having two brains. That's because your left brain lobe and your right brain lobe usually take care of different things you need to think about and do. This drawing shows the outlines of how your real brain looks. Can you point to the left brain lobe and the right brain lobe?

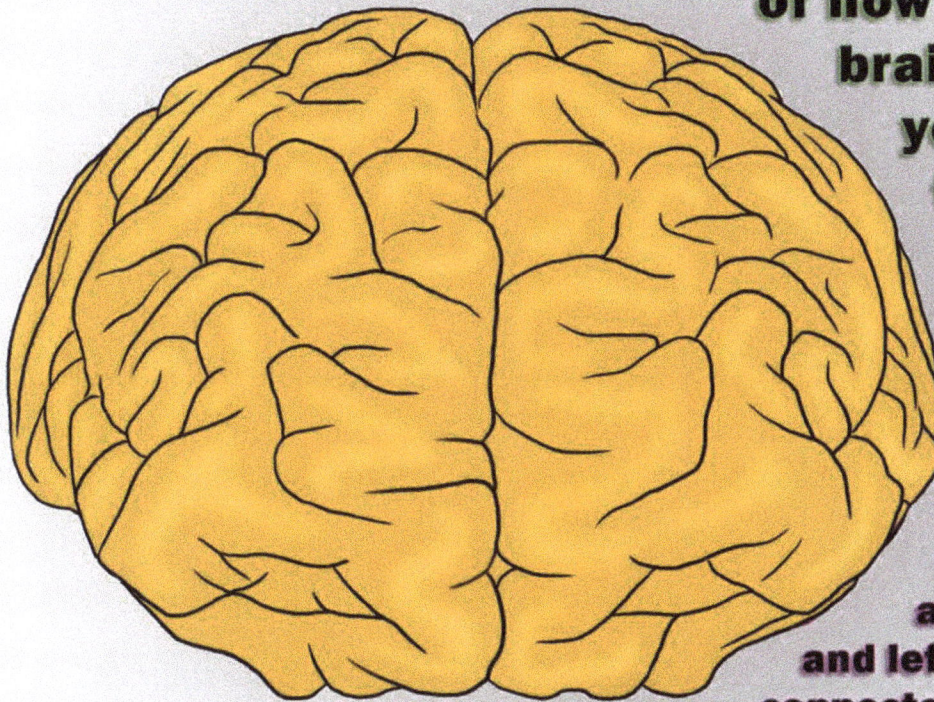

Even though they look sep-arate, your right and left brain lobes are connected right in the middle there. It's the meeting place where they "talk" to each other. How? By sending tiny electrical signals and droplets of special chemicals to each other. You'll read about these chemical messengers in later chapters of this, your interactive brain book.

Now let's take a trip inside your brain.

Meet you brain's chatterbox...
It's your corpus callosum.

Say: KOR - PUS KA - LAH - SUM.

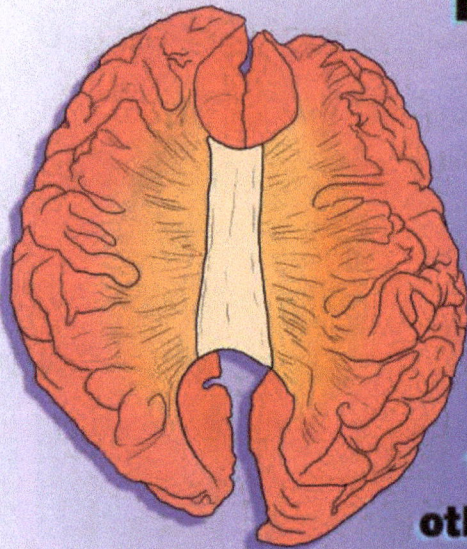

It's where your left and right lobes "talk" to each other.

Your left brain works hard with very sharp thinking. And, also, by figuring things out with numbers. Your right brain is talented and creative. So it helps you make paintings, write poems and compose songs. Together, your two brains help each other get other things done too. **How?**

Each brain lobe gives messages to your corpus callosum. It's that wide white band between both. These messages "talk" through tiny electrical spurts that send tiny wet squirts of special chemicals to your brain's nerve cells, like those you see on the next page.

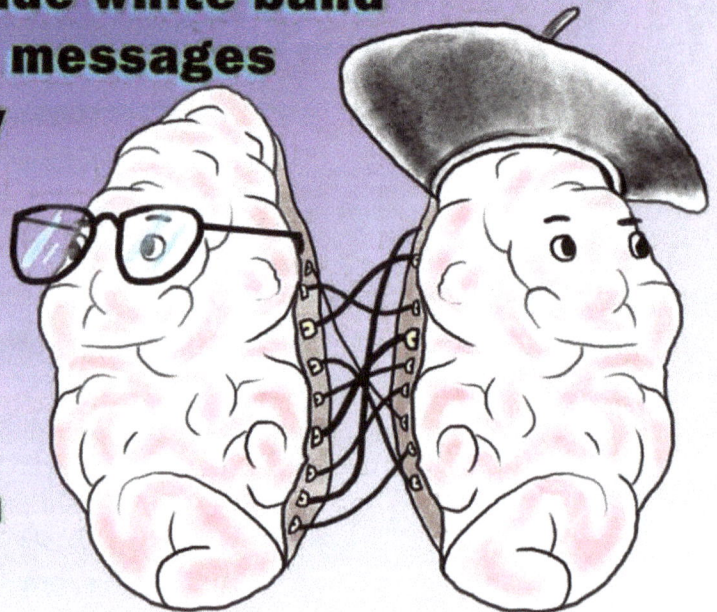

Your left brain loves numbers.

Your right brain loves art and science.

And even your tiniest nerve cells remember to work together.

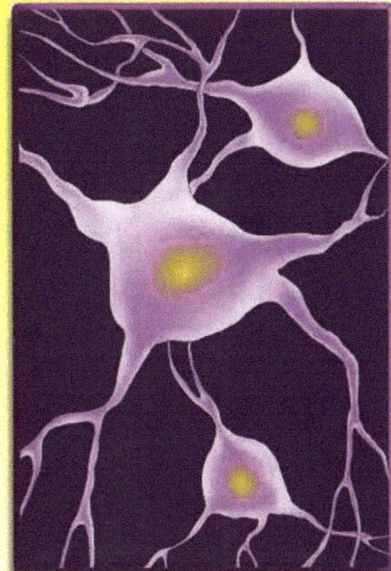

By now you know your real hippocampus is a special memory place inside your brain.

It's called the hippocampus because it's shaped like a seahorse. The word hippocampus means seahorse.

This is what your hippocampus looks like under a very powerful microscope. The colors are added when a brain scientist, who studies it, takes a photo of it.

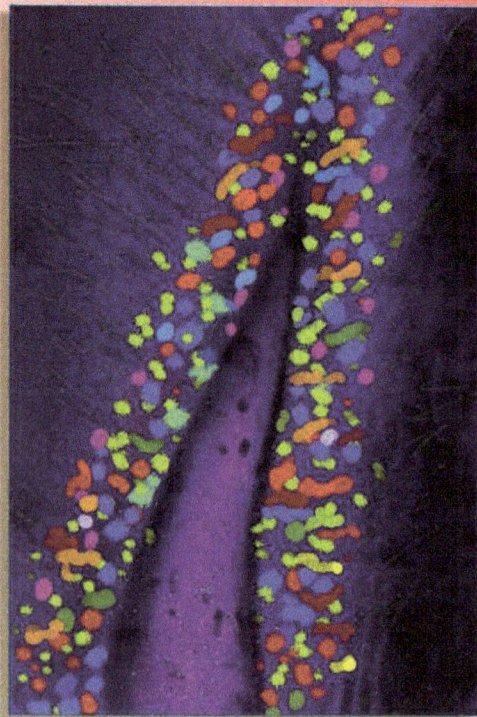

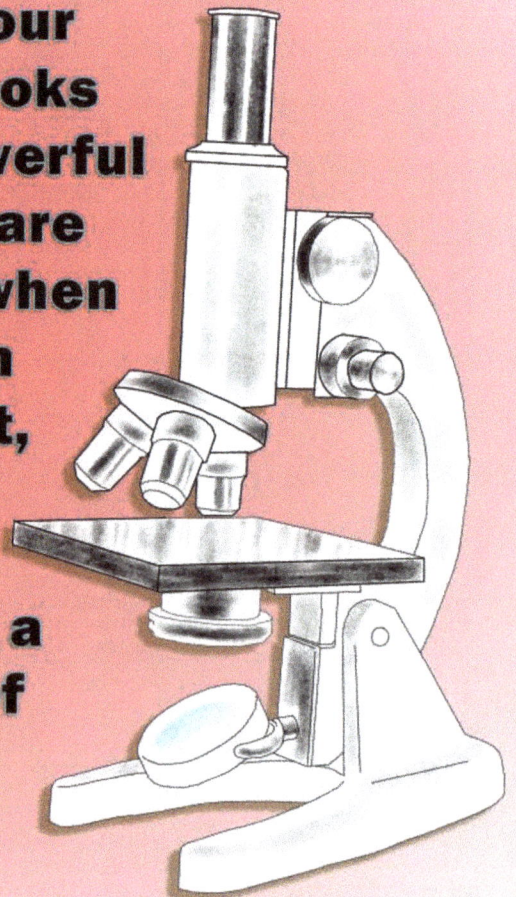

Say: MY - CROW - SKOPE.

Now look at just one hippocampal nerve cell.

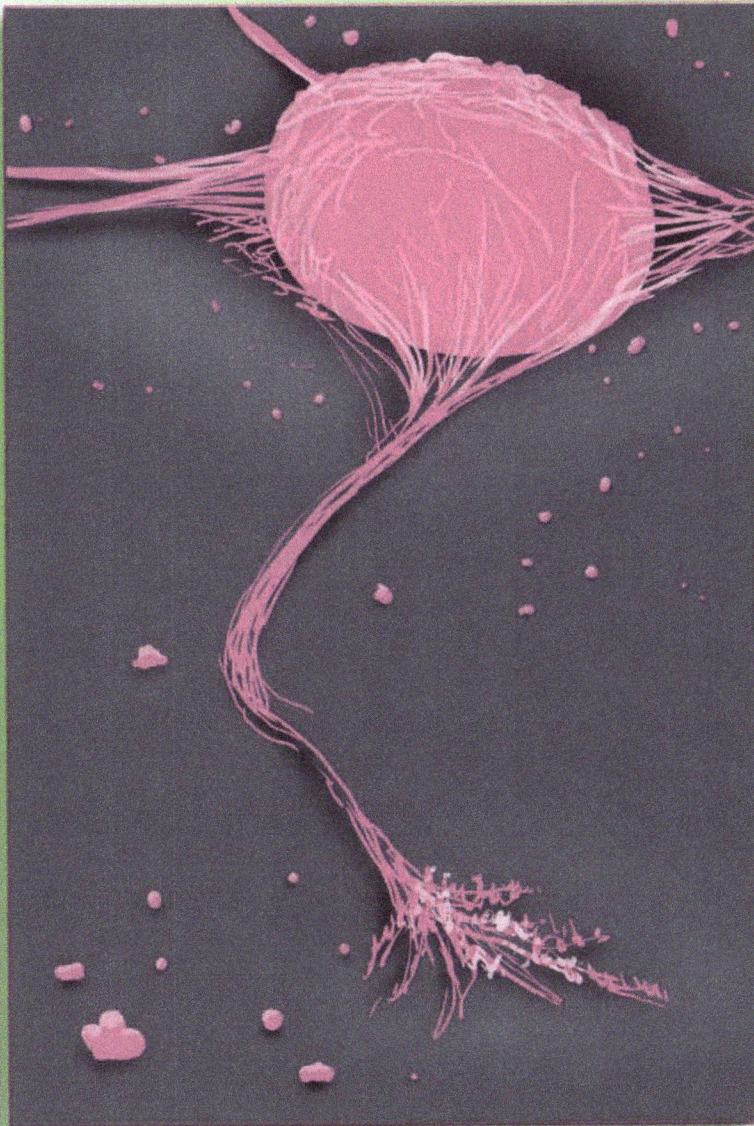

This nerve cell of your hippocampus is magnified, which means enlarged. This nerve cell is called a neuron.

Say: NEW - RON.

You'll learn more about your 100 billion brain neurons in this book's section *Neurons: The Cells of Your Brain.*

Here's a different microphoto of a hippocampus neuron.

This is another beautiful neuron from your hippocampus. You can only see it like this under a powerful microscope. Each of your hippocampus neurons takes a new memory of yours and passes it to another nerve cell like itself. Working together, they take things that happen to you and turn them into memories!

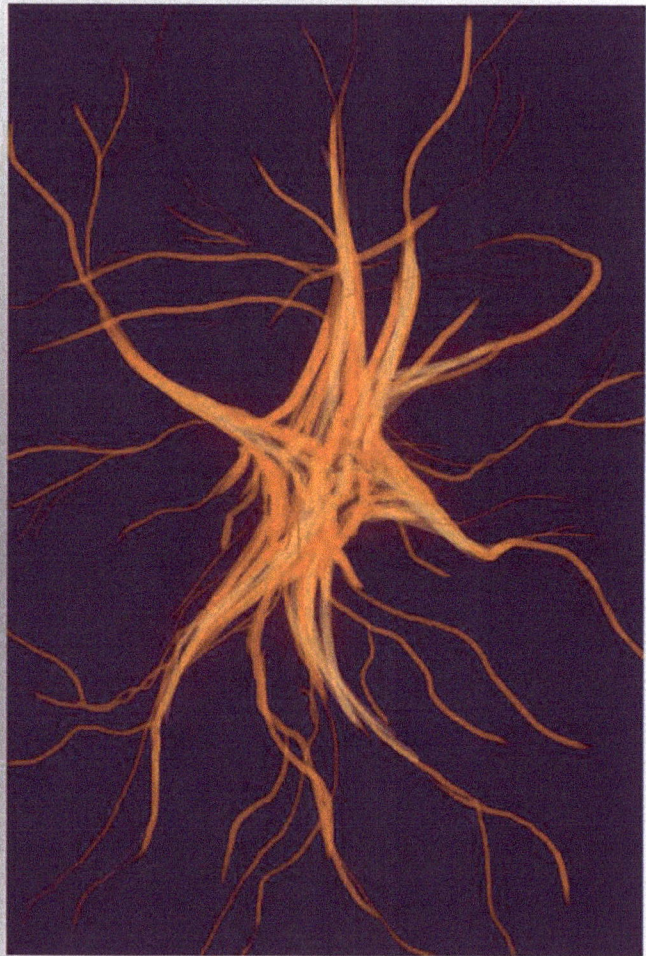

Isn't your hippocampus beautiful?

Your *amygdala* is right there in front of your hippocampus.

See your tiny amygdala? In your brain, it's not really green. It's more like the color of your skin.

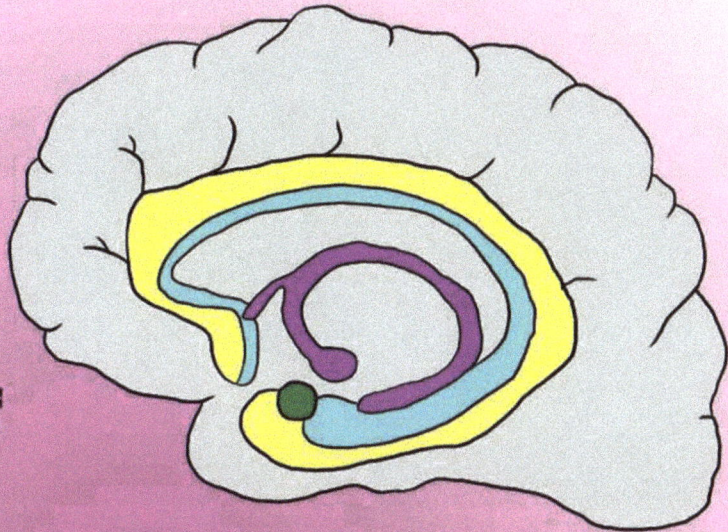

Your amygdala is important because it takes care of some of your strongest feelings. It helps calm you down when you feel bad or angry. And your amygdala warns you to watch out when there's something to be afraid of so you can protect yourself.

Your hippocampus works together with your amygdala to help you remember how you feel.

Brain places to remember

Look at this drawing of your brain.

Now touch your forehead just above your eyebrows. Inside is your *Frontal Cortex.* Say: FRUN - TULL CORE - TEX. It's that part I colored light blue. It helps you do many things.

It helps you get ideas, called *thinking*.
It can make you happy or sad, called *feelings*.
It helps you find memories, called *remembering*.
It also helps you:
▪ move your eyes in different directions;
▪ reach for your toys and for food;
▪ choose the right things to do.

Now find the side of your head, just above either ear. Inside is your **Temporal Lobe.**

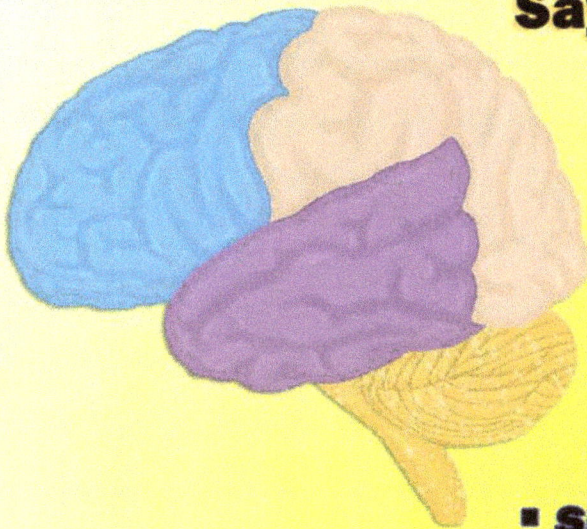

Say: TEM - POR - ULL LOBE.

It's that part colored light purple.

Your temporal lobe helps you:
- *smell* with your nose
- *hear* with your ears
- *speak* with your mouth
- *feel* with your feelings

And that golden "little brain" just below your main brain is your balancing *cerebellum.*

Say: SERA BELL - UM.

Your cerebellum also helps you know where you are, helps you move your muscles, and keeps you balanced as you walk. Together these are called *coordination*.

Say: KO - OR - DI - NA - SHUN

Coordination helps your body parts work together, like when you hit a baseball or play your musical instrument.

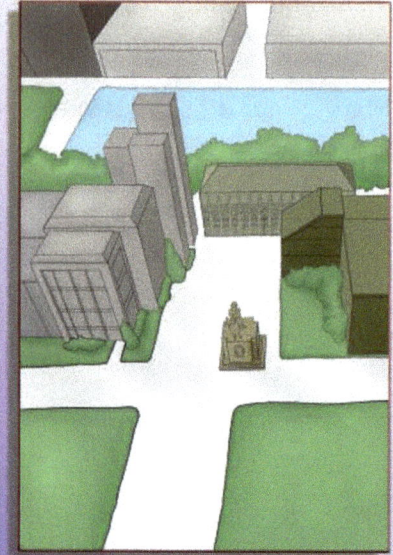

Your cerebellum helps you learn and remember.

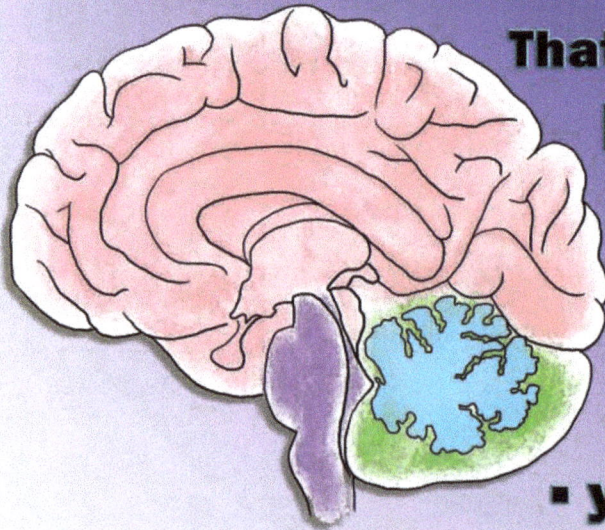

That dark purple part is your **Medulla Oblongata.**

Say: MED - OOH - LAH
OB - LONG - AH - TAH

It sends messages to
• your lungs to breathe
• your heart to beat
• your mouth to swallow • your nose to sneeze

How is it possible for your 3-pound brain to do so much for you?

Neurons: The Cells of Your Brain

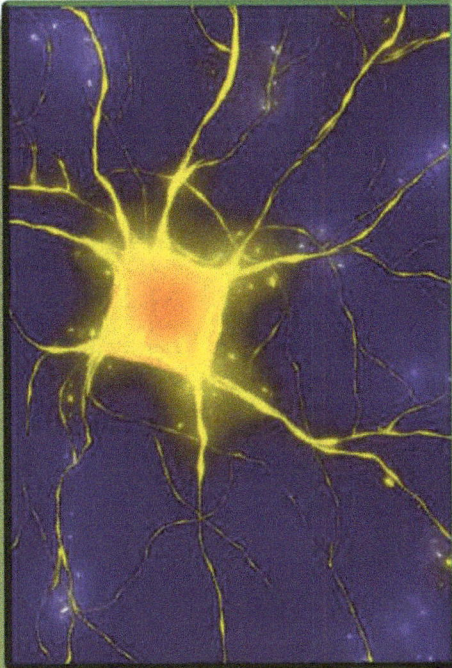

Neurons are nerve cells.

Those thin spidery lines reaching out from the neuron are *dendrites*.

Dendrites kind of "hold hands" with each other. They pass messages to other neurons in your brain. Your neurons are messaging each other all the time, just as if your brain has billions of constantly texting cell phones.

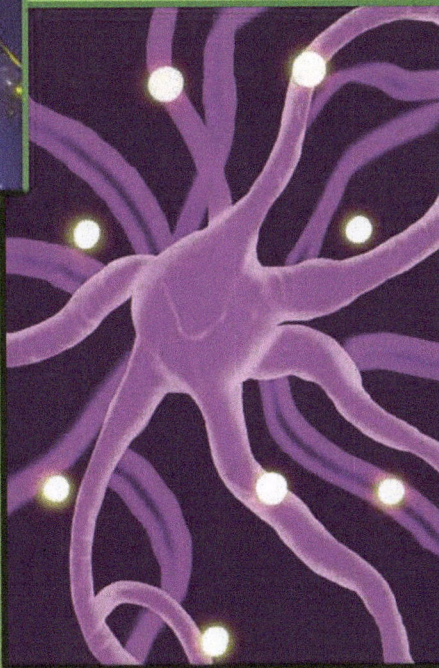

Scientists colored these to show better under a microscope.

The space between neurons is a synapse.

Say: **SIN - APPS.**

Your brain can do so many things for you because the neurons talk to each other across the synapses.

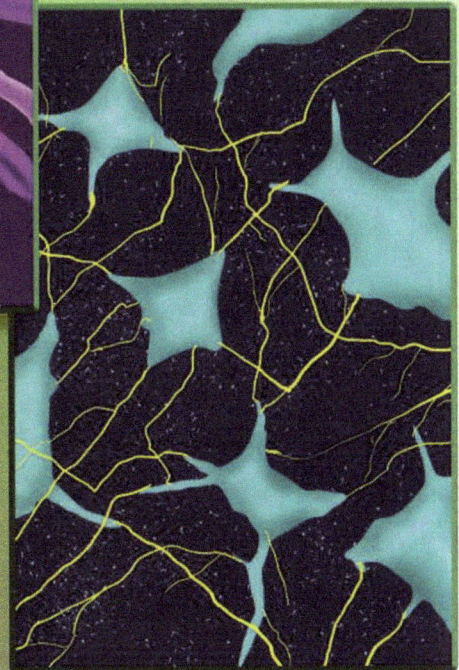

A synapse is the space between the ends of each neuron where brain magic happens.

A synapse is where your neurons message each other with tiny electricity spurts, much tinier than a light bulb. Say: NEW - RON

The electrical action squirts droplets of chemicals to the nearest neuron.   Say: KEM - ICK - KULL

This same thing happens everywhere in your brain between all your billions of neurons. It's your brain's way of "texting" to keep in touch with you and also with every part of your brain itself.

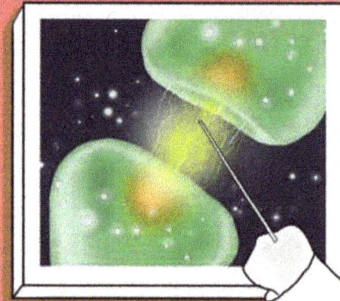

Because of their actions, these droplets are called chemical messengers. Doctors call them *neurotransmitters* because their messages help you think, talk, breathe, walk, laugh, swallow, see, hear, love, learn, remember. And so much more. Say: NEW - ROW - TRANZ - MITT - ERZ

Neurons have long messenging tubes called Axons.   Say: AXE - ONZ

Here is a simple drawing of a neuron.

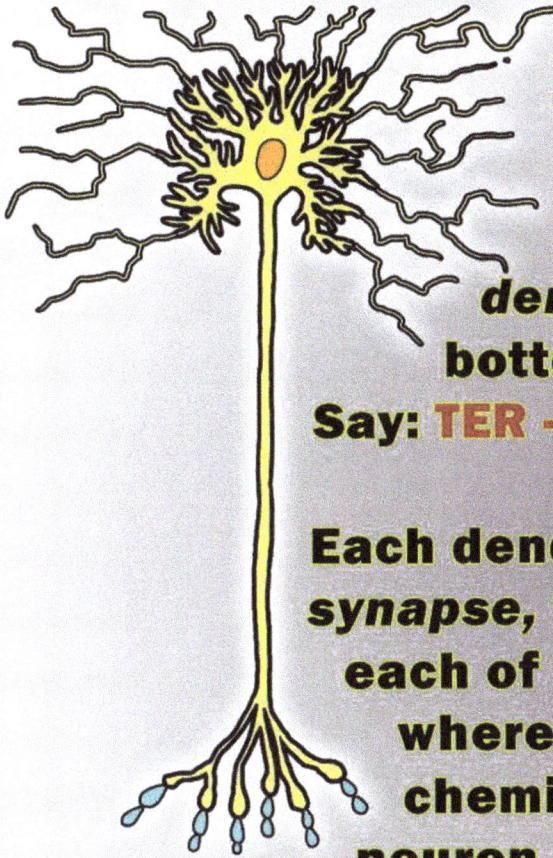

The long part is the *axon*. The round part at the top is the *cell body*. Those branches at the top are the *dendrites*. The branches at the bottom are *terminals*.
Say: TER - MIN - ULLS

Each dendrite reaches out to a *synapse*, that magical place between each of your billions of neurons. It's where tiny electricities squirt chemicals to message the closest neuron. That's how neurons "talk" so they can tell your brain and body:

- what to do
- how to think
- what to feel
- what to remember

Like a symphony orchestra, your neurons act in harmony to make your brain work amazingly.

Make a model neuron.

You'll need some beads and pipe cleaners or bendy wires. The beads can be any shapes or colors. Just string the beads on the bendys and twist them like this drawing. Maybe some young children can help you while you tell them about neurons. Maybe someday you'll make a model brain, too. Maybe someday you'll be a *scientist* who studies the brain. Then you would be called a *neuroscientist*.

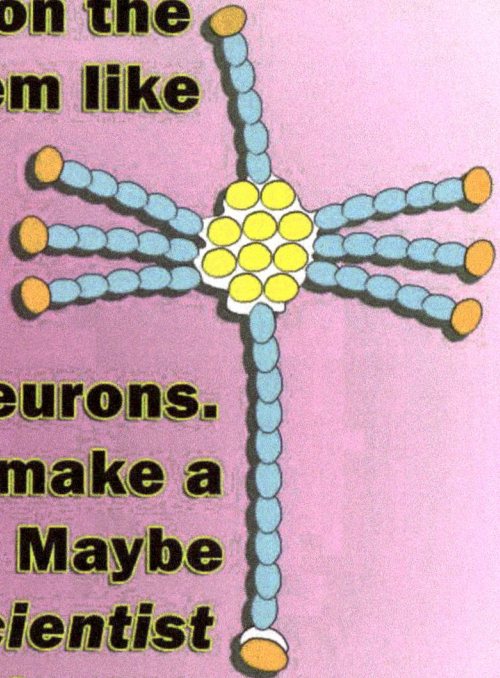

Say: NEW - ROW - SIGH - EN - TIST

Be proud of what you and your brain made. Aren't you and your brain awesome?

Discover your mirror neurons

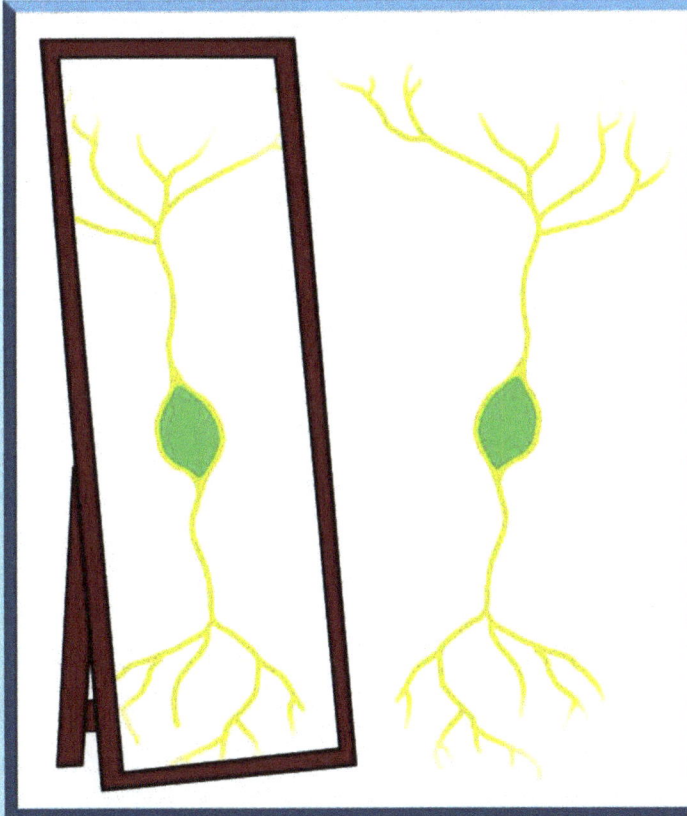

Your mirror neurons make you feel what you see other people are feeling. That's called empathy.

Remember your frontal cortex? It does so much for you, as well as helping you feel sad or happy.

Say: EM - PUH - THEE.

Many of your mirror neurons are in your frontal cortex. There, they help your eyes see what happens to other people. Then your mirror neurons make you feel exactly the same feeling you are watching in someone else. Mirror Neurons make PET Scans of a tennis player and a tennis watcher light up exactly the same.
When both feel the same, that's empathy.

Your mirror neurons make you feel empathy

Having empathy means you care about other people as well as you care about yourself. It's you feeling what others feel from the sound of their voice. Or the look on their face. Or what you feel they feel when they are quiet.

▪ *Empathy* is why you feel like crying when you see something sad happening. ▪ *Empathy* is why you feel like helping when your friend falls down. ▪ *Empathy* is what makes you feel warm and loving when someone is kind to you. ▪ *Empathy* is what helps you be good to yourself, as well as to other people.

Take a look at yourself in your mirror. You're a good kid. Yes you are. That's because you have *empathy*.

And remember: All your brain's neurons send feeling messages to every part of your body, too...

Your neurons make amazing chemicals called neurotransmitters

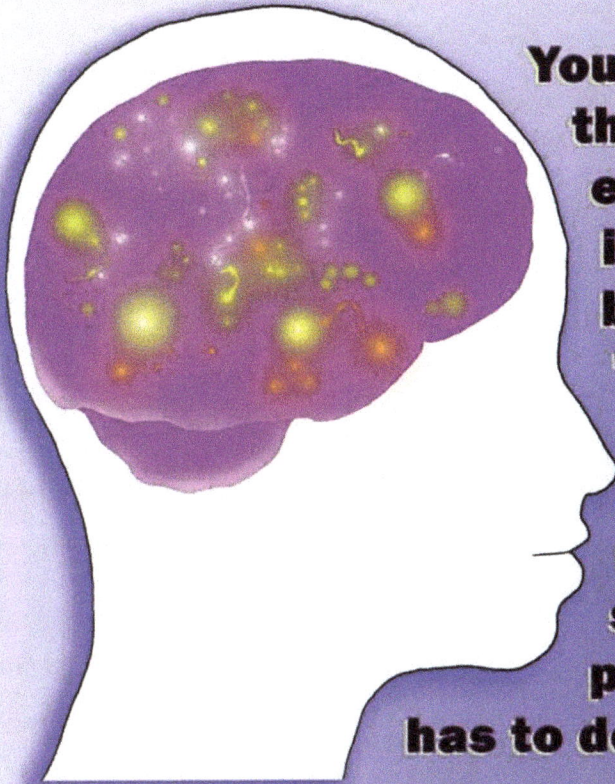

You can also remember them as chemical messengers. That's because it's how your brain's billions of neurons "message" each other. Your neurotransmitters spurt from neuron to neuron, across every synapse, telling every part of your brain what it has to do:

- for your body   - for your feelings
- for your ideas   - for your memories

This picture is from the imagination of the artist. Because he's so excited about how everyone's brain chemistry might look in real life, if you could look inside your brain.

Say: IM - AJ - IN - A - SHUN.

...Squirted from neuron to neuron by mini electrical spurts, like tiny flashes of lightning

Your neurotransmitters are like the directors of movies.

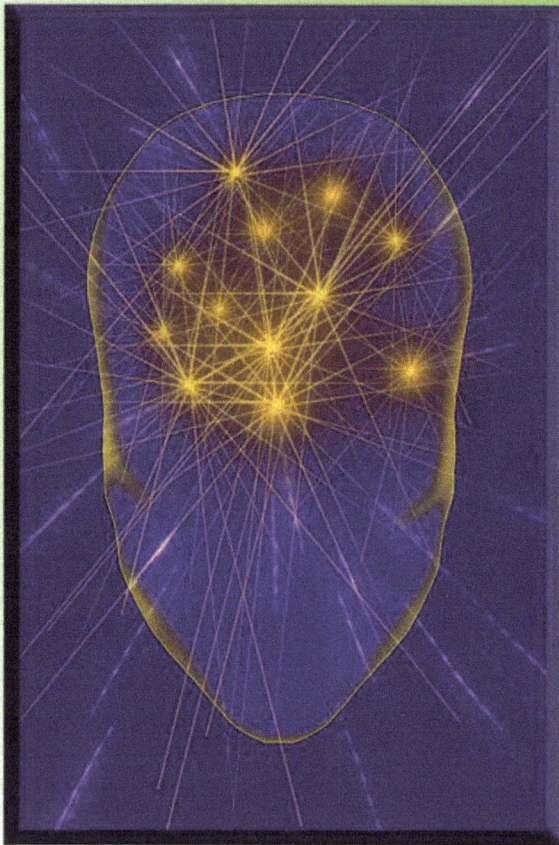

They tell your brain everything it must do to keep you healthy, happy, learning, and filled with memories.

You must remember this:

- From an idea you have...
- Or an action you do...
- Your neurotransmitters light up your brain...

- Traveling neuron to neuron...
- Telling you how to feel...
- Helping you do all the things you do.

Your brain lights up like fireworks when you think up new ideas, and when you feel happy

Remember all the wonderful things going on in your brain at the same time.

Isn't your brain amazing?

Say: UH - MAY - ZEENG.

These are your happiness chemicals:

Dopamine: Say: DOE - PUH - MEEN. Dopamine keeps you in a good mood. It makes you want to learn and pay attention to your homework. It helps you enjoy your piano lessons. It keeps you happy building your sand castle at the beach.

Serotonin: Say: SARA - TOE - NIN Serotonin helps you sleep well. It helps you enjoy the food you eat. It keeps you from feeling too much pain when something hurts you. And it puts you in a "happiness mood."

Oxytocin: Say: OCK - SEE - TOE - SIN Oxytocin is called the "love chemical" because it makes you feel feelings of warm love toward another person. It's the same love chemical that makes a mother feel special love for her newborn baby right after giving birth.

Endorphins: Say: EN - DOOR - FINS Endorphins make pain hurt less or go away. They cause a happy feeling rewarding you for exercising. Creative people like writers, painters, singers, and dancers often feel endorphin-happy. Your brain knows when and how much to squirt these chemicals into the synapses between your neurons. Think happy thoughts and your brain will reward you with happiness chemicals.

Your brain's chemicals send thinking, feeling, and moving messages to all parts of your body.

You have some nerves

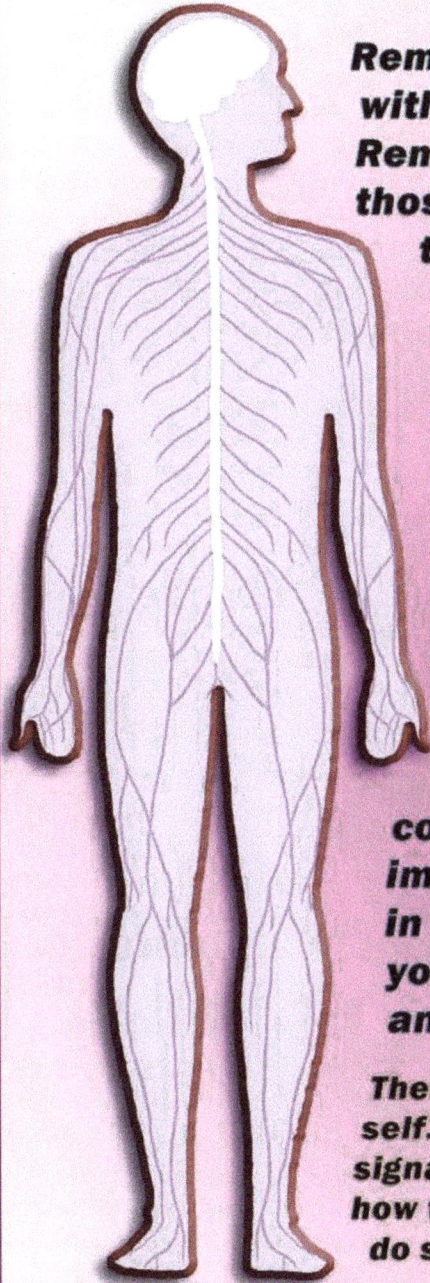

Remember your brain's neurons that connect with each other through tiny electricities? Remember your brain's chemical messengers, those neurotransmitters that tell your body what to do and how to feel?

Now remember, those tiny electrical spurts and tiny chemical squirts travel from your brain all the way down your spinal cord to every other place in your body. That long white tube connected to your brain is your spinal cord.

Together, your brain and your spinal cord are called the central nervous system. Central because your brain and spinal cord are in charge of sending the most important messages to all the far away places in your body...your fingers, your toes, your lips, your nose...everywhere that feeling, moving, and remembering goes.

These nerve connections help you walk and balance yourself. They let you know where you are in the world. They signal to you when something hurts. They tell your muscles how to write, to paint, to play ball, to cook. They help you do so many things, almost anything you can think up.

And remember, they reach your lungs to make them breathe. They reach your heart to make it beat.

Your brain has a master gland called the *pituitary*

Say: PIT - OOH - IT - TERRY

This is a very large picture of your tiny pituitary gland.

It's important because it controls all your other glands that make special chemicals called hormones. It's called "The Master Gland" because it keeps all your body hormones in balance. Your pituitary gland is another wonderful part of your brain.

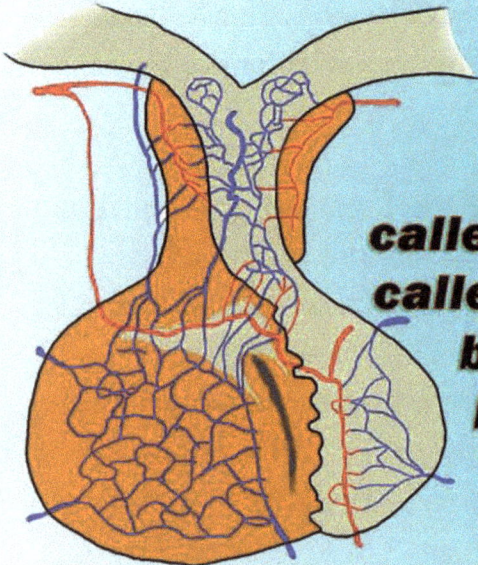

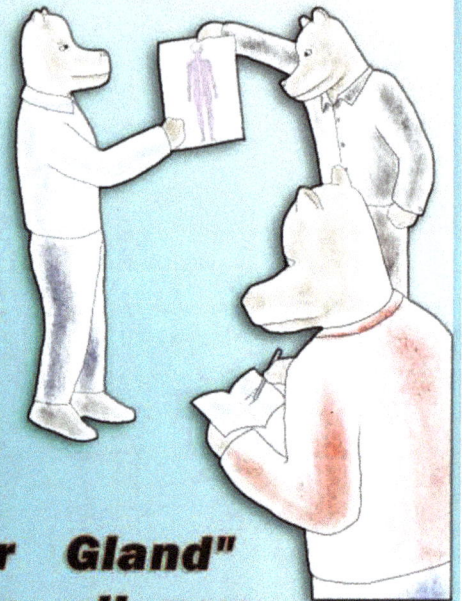

Remember, though tiny as a pea... your pituitary helps your brain keep your whole body healthy.

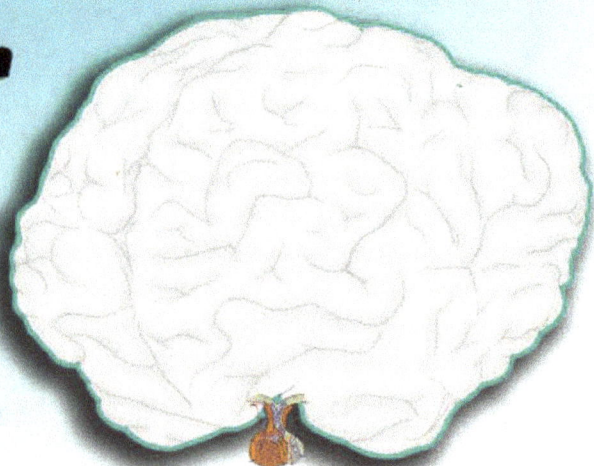

Sometimes doctors do a brain test. It doesn't hurt.

It's called electroencephalogram

Say: EE - LECK - TRO
EN - SEF - UH - LO - GRAM

That's a big word. But it's a simple test of the brain's electricity, which is something like what makes tiny light bulbs turn on.

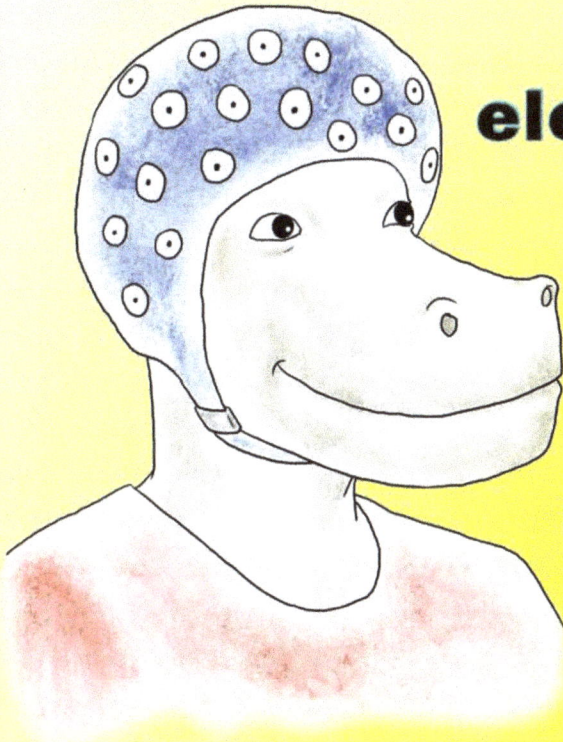

Your brain's electricity makes so much happen all by itself inside your head. And it helps you do all the things you do every day.

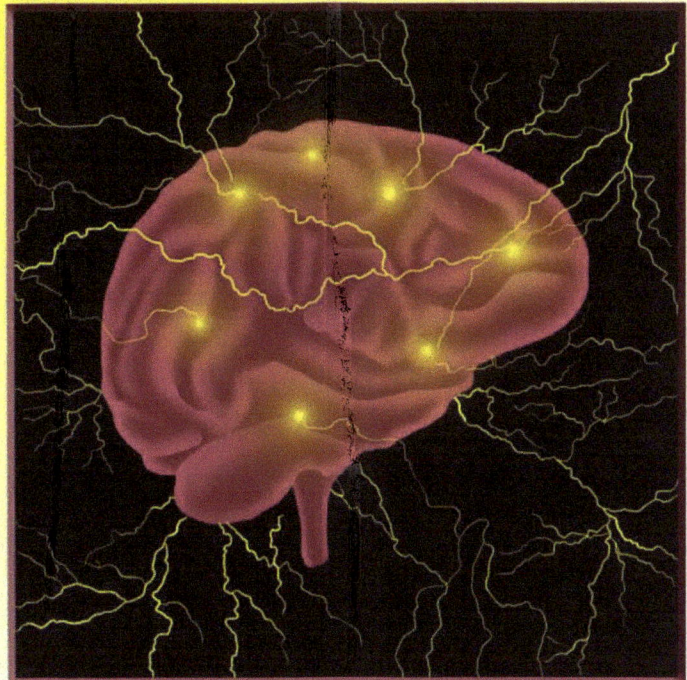

Always remember: Your brain waves make your brain work smoothly for you.

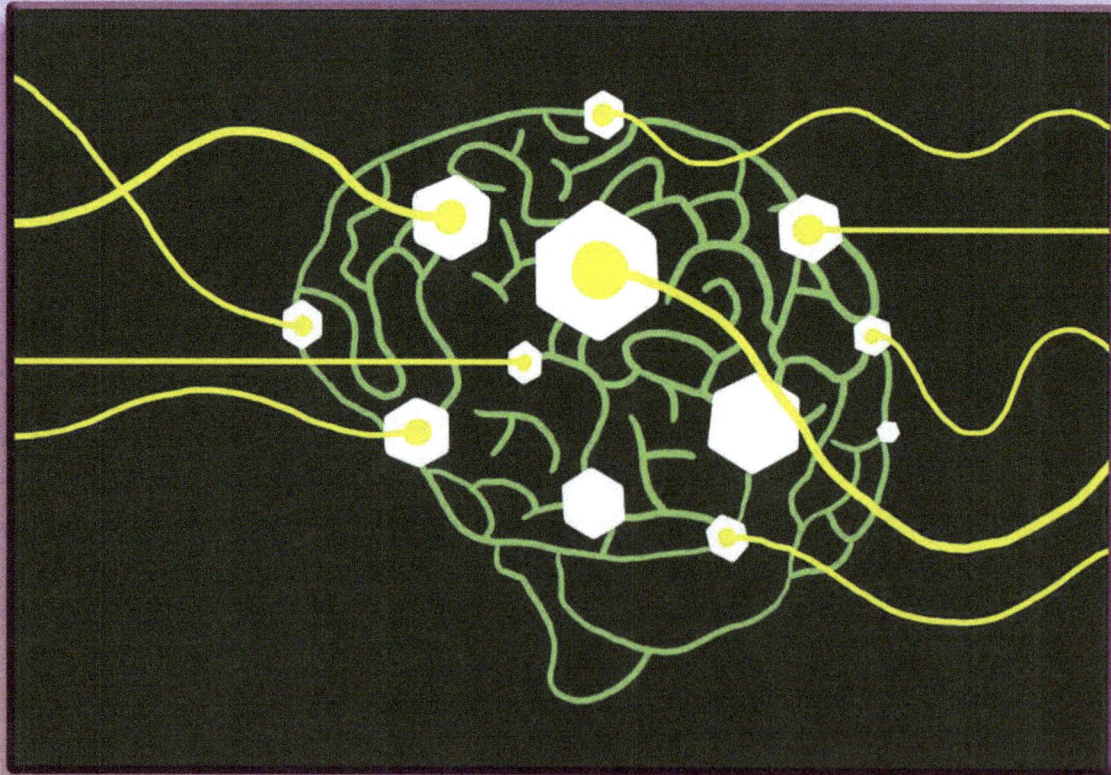

Some people think these brain tests are done by a veterinarian

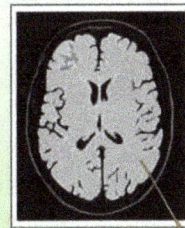

CAT Scan

Say: VET - ER - UH- NARE - EE - IN

That's because a "vet" is a doctor for animals, and the tests are called *PET Scan* and *CAT Scan*, but these are *people brain tests.* They don't hurt.

See that CAT Scan? Your doctor can see that its shape is healthy and that everything in this brain picture is normal.

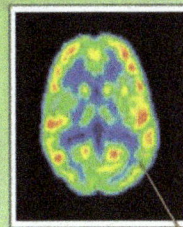

PET Scan

See this PET Scan? It shows healthy chemical activity in your brain. A special glucose is given for this test. (Remember, your brain lives on oxygen and glucose?) These colors show the chemicals called neurotransmitters. In this *PET Scan* the chemicals are working well together.

Do you remember that your right brain helps you make art, music, and inventions?

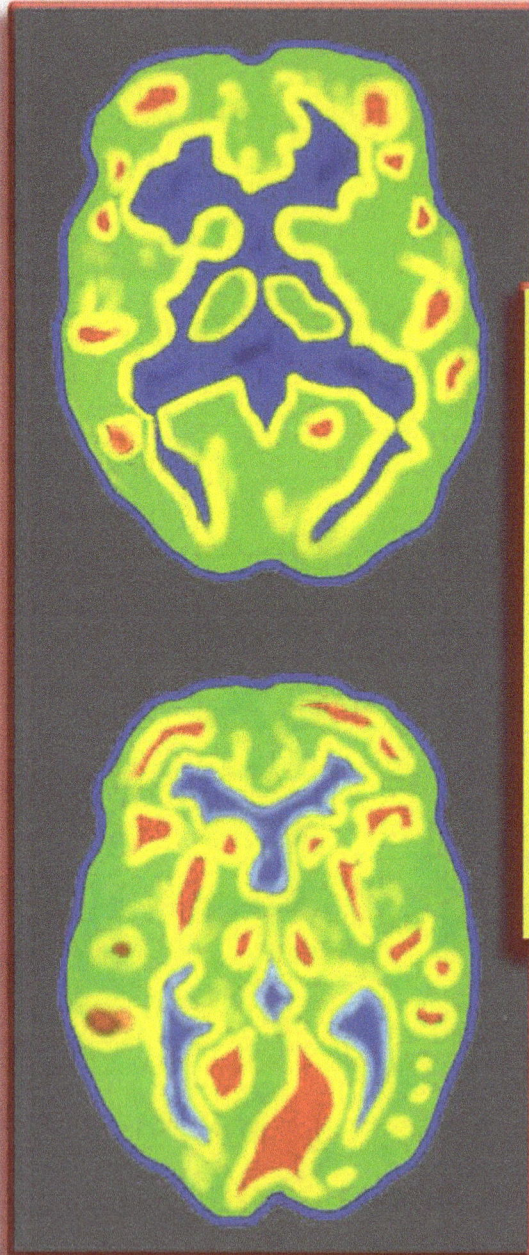

See your brain at rest?

And listening to music?

Brain scientists know that music you love helps your brain grow healthy. It makes you feel good, too.

So play an instrument. Sing. Go to a concert. Listen to music you love.

And if you paint or write poems, your PET Scan will light up just as brightly.

You can also light up your brain by making yourself or someone else feel happy.

The Brainy Bunch

Thousands of people are famous for what their brains helped them do. Some you might know. Some are from long ago. Can you match these brilliant people with what each is famous for? A grown-up can help you learn more about them on the internet.

1. Madame Marie Curie
2. Thomas Alva Edison
3. Florence Nightingale
4. Jonas Salk, MD
5. Amelia Earhart
6. Sigmund Freud, MD
7. Elizabeth Blackwell, MD
8. Anton Chekhov, MD
9. HIPPOCRATES

a. Pioneering American aviator
b. Polio vaccine scientist
c. First woman doctor in America
d. Russian playwright and doctor
e. American lightbulb inventor
f. Radium scientist from France
g. Austrian doctor of memories
h. Greek "Father of Medicine"
i. Pioneering nurse from England

Let's meet some hippocampus scientists.

Camillo Golgi, MD, Italian physician and scientist, discovered how to see the hippocampus under a microscope. He thought neurons were tightly connected like a fishnet, but you know that's not true, so guess what our next genius discovered.

Santiago Ramon y Cajal, MD, Spanish phsician and scientist, discovered that each neuron is a separate cell sending chemical messages to other neurons.

These scientists shared the 1906 Nobel Prize in Physiology or Medicine. They worked on learning the structure of the nervous system, which includes the brain and spinal cord. Dr. Ramon y Cajal is known today as "The Father of Neuroscience."

Your Own Brainy Bunch

Now it's your turn to list all the talented and brainy people you know and admire. They can be family members, classmates, friends. They can be actors, singers, writers, dancers, inventors, comedians, and scientists. Or anybody you've ever heard of whose ways of doing things you admire and feel are brilliant.

About your own wonderful brain

Are you good at doing something? Everyone is. Love it, and keep doing it. It's a special gift.

Are you good with numbers, like Albert Einstein?

Are you good at thinking up inventions, like Thomas Edison?

Do you understand how people think and feel, like Dr. Freud?

Are you curious and excited about science, like Madame Curie?

Do you play a musicl instrument? Sing? Dance? Write poems?

Are you good at making people laugh?

You can be good at more than one thing. If you want to learn to be good at something, write that down, too!

Now you are ready to graduate because of all you have learned so far.

Congratulations!

Helen Borel, PhD

The Hippo Campus Song

Sing to the tune of "Ode to Joy" by Beethoven
(Many versions are on YouTube.com)

Verse
Glory to The Hippo Campus
Where we really learn to spell
Brainy subjects that won't cramp us,
That we can remember well.

Chorus
*Spark that neuron,
Cross that synapse,
Hitch that axon cell to cell,
Make our ideas and our feelings
Ringing clear as a school bell.*

Verses
These are things that we remember:
Brilliance in amazing brains,
January to December,
Brainy memory explains.

Also there's a special section
Every single brain displays;
It's where artists and inventors
Think up new things every day.

Now we know a memory place
Deep inside our busy brains,
'Cause it's shaped just like a seahorse;
Hippocampus is its name.

Since your brain is filled with yearning
for a subject to embrace,
Neuroscience is for learning
of your own Remembering Place.

The Hippo Campus

Always Remember

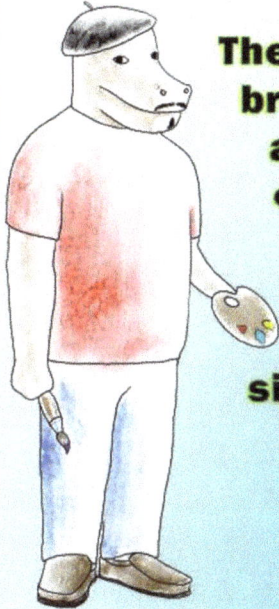

There are many more places in your brain that do special things, such as relaying messages for your:
- mouth to talk
- eyes to see
- ears to hear

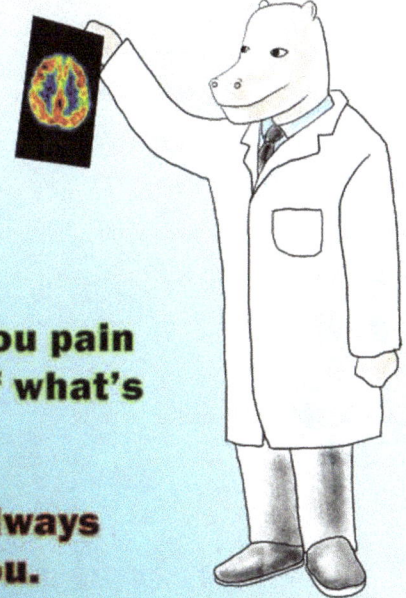

Also, other brain cells send you pain signals to warn you to take care of what's hurting you.

And, be happy that your brain always remembers everything for you.

The Hippo Campus book is only the beginning of your journey into the wonderful world of Neuroscience.

Say: NEW-ROW-SY-ENTS

In case you want to become a
DOCTOR, a NURSE,
a BRAIN SURGEON,
a BIOLOGY TEACHER,
a PSYCHOLOGIST,
a NEUROSCIENTIST,
an ARTIST...
Your brain will help you
succeed in anything
you love to do.

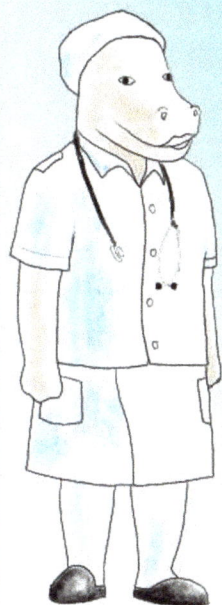

Remember that.

Helen Borel, PhD

Dr. Helen Borel spent her childhood until age 17 writing poetry and playing piano as she grew up in two orphanages. She went on to become a registered nurse, then earned a master's degree in creative writing. She became a doctor in psychoanalytic studies with her own website, PsychDocNYC.com. Always fascinated by the human brain, she is also a writer of books, articles, satire, and more. Dr. Borel lives in New York City in the USA. She dedicates this book to her wonderfully creative grandson, Sean James.

Two BONUS posters just for you! ▶▶

A Place to Remember

2017 The Hippo Campus by Helen Borel, PhD / Fresh Ink Group, publisher

Live Laugh Learn

The Fresh Ink Group

Publishing
Indie Author Services
Video Production
Website Creation
Social Media Management
Writing Contests

☐

Books
E-books
Book Trailers
Writers' Blogs
Podcasts
Amazon Bookstore

☐

Authors
Editors
Artists
Professionals

☐

www.FreshInkGroup.com
Email: info@FreshInkGroup.com
Twitter: @FreshInkGroup
Google+: Fresh Ink Group
Facebook.com/FreshInkGroup
LinkedIn: Fresh Ink Group
About.me/FreshInkGroup

Fresh Ink Group

Cornelius the Cancer Fighting Crocodile takes us on a journey of self-discovery.

With a verse for each letter of the alphabet, the story reassures, enlightens, and empowers youngsters with the message that cancer can be beaten. Cornelius helps friends and family find joy in helping each other through treatment.

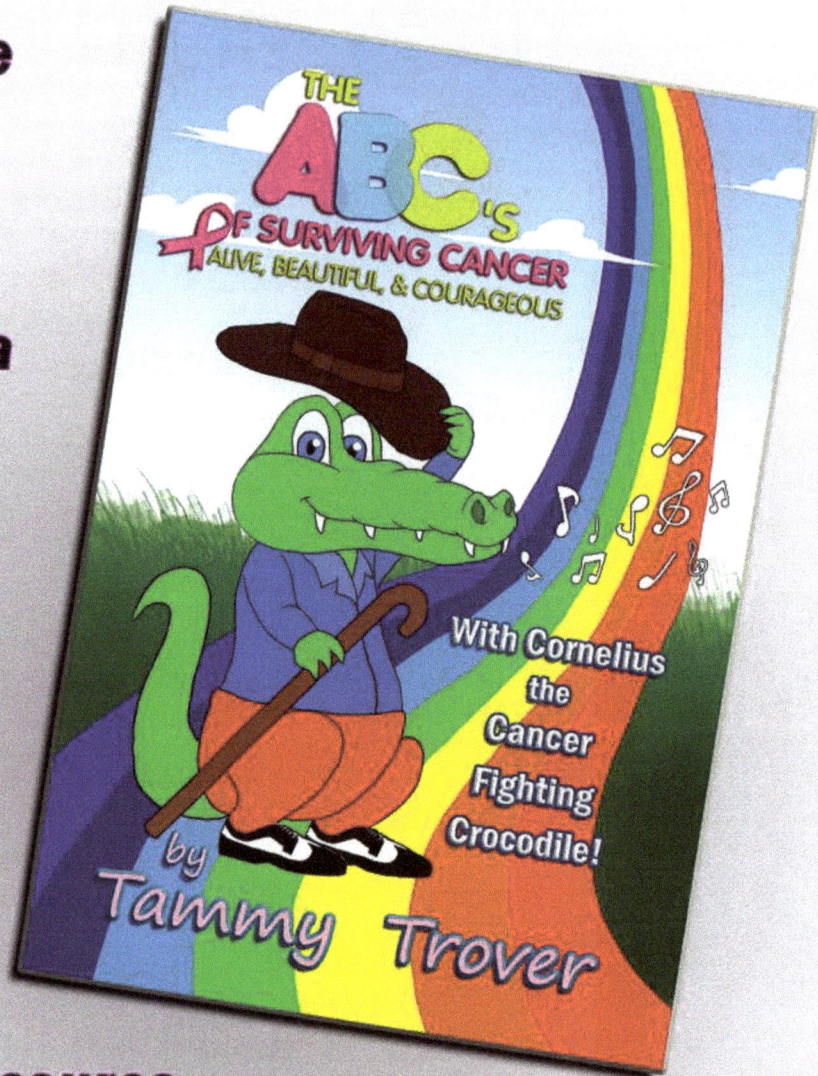

THE ABC's OF SURVIVING CANCER
ALIVE, BEAUTIFUL, & COURAGEOUS

With Cornelius the Cancer Fighting Crocodile!

by Tammy Trover

Fresh Ink Group

www.ingramcontent.com/pod-product-compliance
Lightning Source LLC
Chambersburg PA
CBHW061412090426
42741CB00023B/3491